THE SECRET TO PUPPY LOVE

KAREN PALMER

Dedication

To all the animals that helped me discover my
gifts and to all the people who encouraged me to
share them with the world. I Love you!

Table of Contents

Acknowledgments

I would like to thank my mom and dad for always supporting and encouraging me. I am so grateful for my sister who is my best friend and an amazing blessing in my life. Thank you to my incredible daughter Marissa who inspires me to always do my best. I have tried every day of her life to make the world a little better. I know that I have because she is in this world and she is a beautiful bright light. I want to thank my grandmother who helped me believe I deserve a beautiful life. I want to thank my aunts and uncles who have always been a great source of support and love. I am eternally grateful to all my spirit helpers who guide my words, actions, and footsteps in this world. To all the animals that have literally touched my soul. My life has been forever transformed and I will always speak for the animals. I want to thank my husband; he helped me believe in myself and my gifts. He taught me how to trust and love unconditionally. I want to thank all my friends and family . Thank you to Monika and 99 designs for designing the most incredible cover and to Pamela at Delaney-Designs the creative genius who did the layout for both of my books. I also want to thank all the experts that were interviewed in this book together we are making a difference. Life is beautiful we create it that way.

Introduction

"Never be afraid to do what is right especially if the well-being of a person or animal is at stake. Society's punishments are small compared to the wounds we inflict on our soul when we look the other way."

Martin Luther King, Jr.

The law of attraction has helped millions of people transform their lives including me. I am writing this book as a gift to the world. It is filled with the lessons I have learned and now apply to my everyday life. I will be sharing with you exercises, meditations, and worksheets that will help you have a more spiritual connection with your pet. I have joined with many experts on the subject of law of attraction, mindfulness, Reiki and energy healing to share with you the possibilities for our planet when each person learns these simple lessons and techniques. There will be guided meditations to help you on your journey at www.positivelypetsandkids.com each chapter will explain how to improve your relationship with your pet and this will result in your improving all your relationships. This book will literally change your life and the way you look at your life as well as your pet. I would like to share with people who believe the law of attraction is not religious or spiritual. Please visit www.the-biblespellsitout.com there are many scriptures that explain how the law has worked for centuries. I was raised catholic and when I started to open my mind to these concepts I struggled with my traditional beliefs. I have learned to trust my connection with God and I no longer fear God. Here are some scriptures that help us understand that the law of attraction is very spiritual.

Our thoughts are extremely important.

Where we are today, what our circumstances are, and our level of joy is a direct result of our thoughts.

Proverbs 23:7 "as a man thinketh, so he is."

You can and will change your life by changing your thoughts and actions.

You will be given the strength and wisdom to achieve what you desire.

God is always there to help us and give us the strength we need.

*Psalms 138:3 "On the day I called, you answered me;
you increased my strength of soul."*

With God's help we can do anything.

*Philippians 4:13 "I can do everything through him who
gives me strength."*

Matthew 19:26 "but for God, all things are possible.

If we don't know what to do, God will show us the way.

James 1:5 "If any of you lacks wisdom, he should ask God, who gives generously to all without finding fault, and it will be given to him."

I will uncover hidden secrets that have been proven to transform lives. The possibilities for everyone are incredible if we can learn to raise our vibrations to pure love; which I will explain later in the book. Helping our pets step into their greatness will inspire you to step into your full potential. Our animals radiate pure love energy and the only reason animals that have been domesticated have behavior issues is because they are reading their owner's energy and become a mirror for what the person is experiencing. You can't hide your energy from your pet.

I will share the top behavior issues owners complain about and share simple solutions. 42% of all dog owners admit they have a dog with a problem; this book will not only help solve this problem. It will allow you to wake up to the real reason your pet is in your life. When we step back into our power as a loving leader by sharing pure love and witnessing it on a deeper level in our pets, we will see a huge transformation in our lives; pure and simple.

It is my intention in writing this book that it will resonate with what you already know; your pet is your greatest spiritual teacher. You are about to embark on an adventure as you discover the magic in you and in your pet.

I am a dog trainer, law of attraction coach, Reiki master, animal communicator, and yoga instructor. In this book, I will share all my spiritual gifts to begin a new and innovative way to train dogs. I believe that everyone has spiritual gifts and I am going to teach you to uncover them and share them with the world.

Working with these animals has been a gift and I have learned many lessons that changed my life. Learning to communicate with animals has improved all my relationships. These animals have a beautiful message to share with us and I am honored to be their voice. I look forward to giving you the tools to enjoy meaningful relationships in all areas of your life.

I am committed to helping animals, I donate my time and proceeds from the sales of my products to animal rescue organizations. I train dogs that have been considered unwanted because of the abuse they endured find forever homes. I use the exact techniques I will be teaching you in this book. I have worked with dogs that have been left for dead and used in dog fights to become loving pets. I am also the host of "Positively Pets"a popular radio show with over 25,000 listeners that focuses on people who are helping animals. I have a vision to create a No-Kill Nation for all animals.

3-4 million dogs and cats are killed each year in United States. Those animals don't have the chance to fulfill their purpose and share their loving message. I choose to be a voice for the voiceless and help the forgotten ones.

In my first best-selling book, *"Dogs are Gifts from God"* I take you on my journey from victim to victorious. I am a survivor of domestic abuse, addiction, homelessness, and cancer. I transformed all my tragic to magic. Looking back over my life I understand that the law of attraction was working even in my darkest hours. My most dominant thought during those years was I am not good enough. I continued to experience this in my life until I learned to work with the law deliberately. I am an example of how anything is possible. Working with animals that have been abused allowed me to enhance my spiritual gifts as an animal communicator and truly heal my wounds. I am an advocate for all animals and for women and children that have suffered abuse. My painful experiences have changed my wounds to wisdom and I am able to help many souls. In this book, I will give you my step by step formula that has worked for me and many clients. I will share true stories of empowered relationships and miracles I have witnessed by applying these very teachable techniques. I believe in you and the magic you will uncover using these principles.

I will also be teaching you to use a mindful approach working with your dog. Dogs live in the moment and are not interested about what happened in the past or is going to happen in the future. Humans could really learn a lot from this lesson. I have learned so many important lessons and simple techniques that improved my life and I will be sharing all my *SECRETS* with you. On the back of the book there is a link for my free -companion book. Here you can go along with all the exercises and journal all your success. I will also have videos on my website that follow along with this book. I am setting you and your dog up for a huge transformation.

Have you ever wondered why the same people, pets, or situations are presenting themselves in your life time after time? This is the Universes or God's way of letting you know you have not learned your lesson. With love in your heart, acknowledge this to be true and open to learning the lesson presented to you in this very moment. Once the lesson is learned, the pain from the past can be let go and you can make room to experience new amazing memories that life has to offer. We are all students of the Universe.

What If I was to tell you that your greatest spiritual teacher is in your home and is waiting to teach you the lesson of your lifetime? I have listened and now I am speaking for these animals. I am sharing all that I have learned and please contact me on my blog www.positivelypetsandkids.com/puppy-love-press I am looking so forward to teaching you these amazing skills and helping you discover the Divine in your Canine and in YOU!!!!

"As custodians of the planet, it is our responsibility to deal with all species with kindness, love and compassion. That these animals suffer through human cruelty is beyond understanding. Please help stop this madness."

Richard Gere.

ARE YOU READY?

Chapter 1

WHAT IS THE LAW OF ATTRACTION? & HOW IT CAN HELP YOU AND YOUR DOG?

"In life you get what you put in. When you make a positive impact on someone's life, you also make a positive impact in your own life."

Unknown

T he law of attraction asserts that a person's thoughts attract objects, people, situations, and circumstances; both negative and positive. It simply states that the law will bring you whatever you think about most.

Thoughts become charged when you desire something-you feel emotion each time your mind thinks about what you desire. If you feel happy and excited at the thought of having what you are thinking about; and *believe you deserve it* you will speed up the manifestation process. Your excitement and happiness will be a match for what you desire. However, if your thoughts and beliefs are negative and you are thinking of what you don't want to happen you will be a match for that. *Whatever you are thinking and believing will happen is what you create.*

The law of attraction works in response to thoughts that have become energized. If you place your attention and focus all your energy on what you do want; you will bring it to your life. You must be careful and watch your thoughts because whatever you think about most becomes your most dominant thought. Please understand repetitive negative thoughts that are charged with the emotion of fear can bring you what you fear also.

When you truly understand the fundamentals of the law of attraction and place your focused attention on the results you want to accomplish you will succeed. Please don't put any attention on the behavior you don't want and you will notice things changing right away.

Who Can Use the law?
How do I apply it with training my dog?

Anyone can work with the law of attraction and achieve whatever they desire. You will have a well-balanced and good mannered dog. You can accomplish it easily. Here is an example of how you can use the law with dogs.

1. The dogs in our life are blessings and want to please us. They need clear direction on what you would like them to do. Set your intention for example to have a dog who will peacefully greet guests as they enter your home.

2. Please understand a dog who is barking is using his bark to get your attention. The dog needs to receive plenty of exercise. The dog is nervous, anxious, or upset. If we yell at the dog to stop the dog will feed on our negative energy. It is important that we stay calm, loving, and focus our attention on the desired result and we establish that we are the loving leader. I will offer you more tips and tools about this in later chapters.

3. Use a clear signal or sound that gets the dog's attention back onto you and treat for positive behavior.

4. A tool that I use when training is called a slip collar. This is one of the best tools to get your dog's attention quickly. I highly suggest to all my clients to have a slip collar. They can be purchased at www.dogsupplies.com It is important that you use a slip collar correctly many people call them a choke collar. It will only choke your dog if you are using it incorrectly.

5. Simply slip the loop over your dog's head and slide the attachment to hold securely on the top of the head. The lead bottom should be just under the chin, so you can quickly get your dog's attention. Take your dog for a walk using this tool and mindfulness; which we will discuss in later chapters. Set your dog up for success I will share more tips for this later in the book. Here is a beautiful meditation you can do before going for a walk. It is recorded at www.positivelypetsandkids.com

Top Tips for Being a Loving Leader

1. Teach your dog the command, sit and stay. Treat when you get the desired result and continue to do this for a few days using hand signals and the words sit and stay.

2. Next, have your dog sit and stay while you prepare its food. Make sure it sits calmly and just watches what you are doing. Give lots of praise and when you are ready place the bowl on the floor a few feet from your dog. Continue to have your dog stay until you give the signal or say it is okay.

3. Please, be sure that you *always* have your dog sit and stay at the door before you leave the house. You are showing that you are the leader. It is a good idea to open the door while you have your dog on the leash and correct quickly if it tries to lunge toward the door. This may take a few times or it may happen on the first try. Please stay calm and positive, visualize the result you would like to see, add an affirmation or a positive thought. Your dog will be so proud and remember to give your dog a new challenging job or fun trick every day. If a dog does not have a job it will become self-employed. This is when you have more issues. Dogs want to please us; but we need to give very clear direction to get the behavior we want.

4. When you are out on the walk, make sure your dog is beside you or behind you. Give a sound signal when you feel your dog is pulling. You will set the pace and correct if the dog tries to pull you. Drop your shoulders and walk calmly and relaxed. We will discuss how to enjoy a mindful walk in Chapter 7.

The most beautiful people we have known are those who have known defeat, known suffering, known struggle, known loss, and have found their way out of the depths. These people have an appreciation, a sensitivity, and an understanding of life that fills them with compassion, gentleness, and a deep loving concern. Beautiful people do not just happen.

Elisabeth Kübler-Ross

Lessons from Chapter One

In this chapter we learned about focusing on what you want here are a few exercises you can complete to accomplish great results.

1. What is one area of your life that you are happy or pleased with? Write it down here:

_____

_____

_____

_____

_____

2. Why? What about this area makes you happy?

   What about this area of your life is aligned with how you imagine life **should** be?

_____

_____

_____

_____

_____

3. What is an area of your life that you desperately want to change? Write it down here:

_____

_____

_____

_____

_____

4. Why? What about this area makes you unhappy?
   What about this area of your life is different from how you
   imagine your life **should** be?

_____

_____

_____

_____

_____

Chapter 2

HOW EXPERTS USE
LAW OF ATTRACTION?

An interview with law of attraction guru; *Natalie
Ledwell is an author, speaker and Life Improvement
Crusader. She has positively impacted the lives of millions
of people around the world by empowering them to achieve
their dreams through her life changing online programs.
You can find out more about Natalie at*
www.mindmovies.com

Natalie shared with me that when she saw the movie, "The Secret" it completely changed her life; something clicked and it finally made sense to her. She was excited to see how simple the principles were and that she did not have to get hung up on how it was going to happen. She understood she just needed to be very clear about what she wanted and take one action step in that direction. Her story is so inspiring. Natalie, her husband, and her business partner created the mind movies; which are visual photographs, with inspiring music and positive affirmations. The Mind Movies has reached over a million people and Natalie is living her dream life. She is the host of a very popular online show called, "The Inspiration Show" she interviews successful people and shares the techniques people use daily to stay in the vibration of success. This book is filled with these tips and principles based on many of these techniques.. Natalie is a perfect example of how the law of attraction works. She also rescued a dog named Bella and she lives in deep connection with her dog. They meditate together and enjoy mindful walks many times a day. Bella is a very calm and loving dog who goes to work with Natalie and travels beautifully. Natalie uses these principles and she knows her energy effects Bella. They are both radiating pure love out into the world. Natalie has recently manifested another of her lifelong dreams; she published her first book, "Never in your Wildest Dreams". She believes she received a massive download from source as she wrote her book and envisioned how it can help the world. I highly recommend this book. I will have a place on my website where you can develop your own 'Mind Movie' with your pet and accomplish results faster. http://www.mindmovies.com/products/order_mindmovies.php?25707

Here is the link to get her book http://www.mindmovies.com/niywd/bonusgifts.php?25707 I am so grateful for attracting Natalie in my life she has helped me see how fun and simple life is, I love her book and encourage you to get a copy. It is wonderful.

An Interview with a Goddess

Cynthia Occelli is the author of "Resurrecting Venus" and host of Hay House online show of the same name. Cynthia explains to us that all animals are divine essence. She believes that everything issues from the creative mind. Everything on some level is divine. Cynthia is another great example; she has a spiritual connection with all three of her dogs. She has a border collie; who she describes as brilliant. A shih tzu; who is a lap lion and healer and a maltese; who has plenty to say. Each animal is part of her family and have helped her through many challenges and difficulties. She shares many of these amazing stories in her book and on her blog post. I am extremely grateful, Cynthia was guided into my life and the wisdom she shares with the world is magical. Her online radio show is always inspiring and empowering.

She discussed what she thinks the law of attraction is; she explains there are two worlds, the physical world and the energetic world. The thought needs to come first which is an energy that will create the physical which she calls inspired action, with these actions the Universe will conspire with us to help us co-create the reality. We will create what we are investing the most energy in, physically and emotionally. In chapter three, we will discuss the role emotions play. Cynthia also shares that we are using the law of attraction all the time; we are using it consciously or by default. We have to begin to understand there are some things in the world that are out of our control and we need to trust there is something bigger happening and have faith. Then there are other parts that we can change which are our thoughts, beliefs, and emotions. This is how we are powerful co-creators in the world. To learn more about Cynthia please visit www.cynthiaoccelli.com *I highly recommend Cynthia's book, online show, and blog post. She really changed my life and helped me remember I am the most powerful person in my life. I feel more confident and courageous than I ever have in my life. I am so thankful I attracted Cynthia and Natalie in my life; what a blessing.*

> *"Energy of a certain quality or vibration tends to attract energy of a similar quality or vibration. Thoughts and feelings have their own magnetic energy which attracts energy of a similar nature".*
>
> *Shakti Gawain*

Lessons from Chapter 2

Here are a few exercises that will help you with your goals.

1. Imagine this: Your life is ALREADY exactly the way you want it to be.... How do you describe it?

   _____

   _____

   _____

   _____

   _____

2. If someone asked you, "What have you been up to lately?" then how would you answer?

   _____

   _____

   _____

   _____

   _____

3. What is the essence of what you're seeking to achieve with these lessons?

   _____

   _____

   _____

   _____

   _____

Chapter 3

Chapter 3

THE ROLE OF EMOTIONS

"Know that the same spark of life within you is within all our animal friends, the desire to live is within all of us. We are connected; God weaves a beautiful tapestry; the thread that brings us together is the animals."

Anonymous

The Role of Emotions: Another extremely important part of working with these principles is to understand how your mood affects your ability to manifest the results you desire.

Your mood is the best indicator of your emotions. Everyone feels emotions in various bodily sensations. Your emotions can affect the way you make a decision. There are six basic types of emotions.

1. Love
2. Surprise
3. Happiness
4. Fear
5. Sadness
6. Anger

You must learn to identify the state of mind that is best suited for making decisions. Learning to understand your emotions can help you in all areas of your life. I hope you are beginning to see how helping your dog step into its greatness is also helping you. We are connected and the animal in our life is there for specific growth lessons. If you can learn to express your emotions in a calm and peaceful way, life will be much easier and your relationship with your dog will be more fulfilling.

Expecting to receive what you desire is vital in getting it. A heightened sense of expectation intensifies the vibration of thought when you dare to expect what you desire. Allowing yourself to feel a sense of expectation reinforces the attraction or the pull of it to you. Visit www.positivelypetsandkids.com to listen to a wonderful visualization on using your emotions as a guide to accomplishing your desired results. There are Four Basic Techniques for manifesting. I will share many true stories of how I used these techniques to help incredible dogs who had severe abandonment issues and many other issues in chapter 6.

Four Basic Techniques for Manifesting a Peaceful Greeting for your Guests

1. Focus on all the abundance and blessings in your life. Focus on the qualities you love about your dog. Where focus goes energy flows, you will see your dog exhibiting the qualities you focus on the most. Use emotionally charged positive thinking and spends a few minutes each day just thinking about the behavior you would enjoy experiencing with your dog.

2. Set your intentions in writing; put it in a place where you can see it often. Be very specific and make it very clear in your statement; "what do you want"? An example is: I am training my dog to be calm and welcome my guests peacefully in my home. Notice, I did not focus on what I don't want the dog to do. (For example no barking, jumping, or rude behavior.) Now take a few moments to think about the emotions you will feel when your dog accomplishes these results. Continue to do this daily and you will see amazing benefits.

3. Be ready to receive and feel the emotions that come with getting your desired result. (For example think of how happy and proud you will be to have guests over and a well-behaved, loving dog sitting by your side ready to greet your company.

4. Develop an attitude of gratitude and offer appreciation often. Dogs respond extremely well to kindness and gratitude. Each day, spend about 3-5 minutes counting your blessings in your life and begin with your amazing dog and new spiritual teacher.

My good friend and fellow dog trainer Michelle shares how to avoid dog bites. You will learn how dogs are communicating with us.

About Michelle Huntting

While working in the Christian education field, Michelle pursued her interests with dogs by training as a hobby. Soon she started a pet sitting business and eventually opened a holistic pet food store and training facility in Ankeny, Iowa. Michelle earned a certification through the Certification Council for Professional Dog Trainers, and years later, earned a certification through Animal Behavior College. Michelle graduated with honors in 2012 earning her bachelor's degree, and is currently pursuing her graduate degree. Michelle owns and operates Miss Belle's Etiquette School for Dogs; her training business in North Carolina. During her life experiences of training dogs, Michelle realized the need for higher academic standards in the Dog Training field. Due to her passion for education, she opened Kenyon Canine Institute, an online education for professional trainers that offers college level training courses. She also hosts a popular internet radio show, Dog Talk. She is currently working on a book about leash walking schedule to come out in September 2013. Michelle enjoys spending time with her three dogs Boy, Morgan, and Belle. She volunteers her time as a therapy team with her dog Boy, and also volunteers with Doggone Safe's "Be a Tree" program, teaching children about dog bite prevention.

www.missbelles.com

www.kenyoncanineinstitute.com

Dog Bite Prevention; Learning to Speak Dog

Learning how to prevent a dog bite is not a secret code that needs to be deciphered. In most cases, dog bites can be prevented. It really is as simple as learning a few things that a dog is communicating to you. In other words, it's learning to speak his language; learning to speak dog.

Dogs obviously (although I think it would be awesome) can't verbalize, "Wow, I am really uncomfortable; please remove this child from my face." But your dog is communicating this nonverbally with his body language.

The behaviors that are communicated by dogs which reveal he is uncomfortable are called displacement behaviors. When I was driving into the grocery parking lot, a lady was coming out of the store, so I stopped my van to let her pass. As she walked past me, for whatever reason, she took her hand up to her face and scratched her cheek. She obviously wasn't scratching because her face itched, she was scratching because she was uncomfortable. Displacement behaviors are normal behaviors, but happen out of context. Some examples would be; if a dog were to shake off, even though he didn't have a bath, if he were to lick his lips, but there is no food around, or he yawns when there was a camera in his face. Displacement is contextual.

In one of my Puppy Kindergarten classes, a student complained her dog was scratching frequently. The owner said, "I *don't know why she keeps scratching?*" She said she had checked for fleas, the dog is on a good diet, etc. I observed her with the puppy and noticed every time the she said a cue; sit, or down, the puppy scratched. I explained the tone of the pet owner's voice when saying the cue was a little sterner than her puppy enjoyed.

I encouraged the owner to say the cue; sit, or down, in a softer tone and the puppy stopped scratching after the first cue. It's amazing what we can learn if we just "listen."

What are some displacement behaviors?

- Licking the mouth
- Self grooming
- Sniffing the ground
- Scratching
- Yawning
- Turning the head to the side
- Shaking off

When a pet owner sees their dog showing signs of displacement, it is important to adjust the environment and that doesn't (although it can) necessarily mean that the dog must be removed from the situation. Adjusting the environment could be as simple as helping the child to gently pet your dog on his side rather than his head. It's important to continually "listen" to your dog. We want to remove him from the uncomfortable situation all together if it's just too much for him. You can watch for several displacement behaviors, signs of stress and also be in tune with what your dog is feeling.

What are some signs of stress?

- Sweaty paws (you will see paw prints on the floor)
- Excessive shedding
- Heavy panting
- Pupils dilated
- A lot of blinking
- No blinking
- Tension in eyes and mouth
- Not able to take food

Knowing your dog is just as important as watching for signs of displacement and stress. I train therapy classes for Miss Belle's® and we teach a lot about knowing our dog, because a therapy team can find themselves in a variety of situations. Some situations are uncomfortable, so it's important for the handler or pet owner to know their dog. Is this a situation that will stress my dog? If so, it's important to remove your dog from the situation which is causing stress.

Did you know that dogs don't enjoy hugs? Yes, I am serious. When watching dogs interact have you ever seen one throw his paw up around the other just to show affection? This is not a dog behavior. I am very thankful that dogs are tolerant with us and put up with our humanness. Although most dogs tolerate hugs, there are a few that don't. There are times when a dog has communicated he was very uncomfortable to the owner. The owner didn't "listen" to him saying he was uncomfortable with hugs. And then on the 40th hug the dog decided he needed to do something about it; which could mean an air snap, a growl, or maybe even a bite. This is why we teach children about dog bite prevention and we encourage them not to give dogs hugs. There are many other fun and safe activities with dogs for children to enjoy.

Some good resources: www.doggonesafe.com and also www. familiypaws.com

Do not pet a dog if you see these types of stress behaviors:

- Half moon eye, also called whale eye. This is when you will see the whites of the eyes as the dogs eyes are turned to the side. Usually the half moon eye is followed by a bite. If you see this behavior it is a good sign to walk away.

- Dog is stiff. A loose dog is a happy dog; if the dog's body is stiff he is uncomfortable.

- Dog's tail up and stiff

- Dog is holding foot up (it will be a quick foot pop)

- Dog leaning forward

How you approach a dog is crucial. Think about the context of the human world. If you were to meet me for the first time, although I am a friendly person, I wouldn't enjoy you coming within two feet of my face and then giving me a hug. I would appreciate some space with the introduction, and so do dogs. I would also appreciate a hand shake, that's polite in our world right? Being polite in the dog world involves smell. Being polite to a dog, is giving him some space. Place your hand out for the dog to smell. Allow him to come to you. You know, like the kissing rule of 80/20. The guy leans in 80 percent of the way and waits for the girl for the other 20. Allow him to come to your hand and sniff you. Sniffing allows a dog to gain all sorts of information about you; what you had for breakfast, if you are a boy or a girl, and if you have pets at home. After you have let him have a good sniff and he's acting relaxed, then it's okay to pet him.

Petting a dog one hand is enough, two hands is simply too much. Pet him on the side of his body or neck. When petting, be sure to either squat or stand at the dog's side; not directly facing him. Never lean over a dog, as this is a threatening position for him. Most dogs enjoy nice long strokes versus heavy patting.

As a pet owner, it is important to be your dog's advocate. Watch his body language, protect him. If you know he will be uncomfortable, walk away. Students going through therapy training at Miss Belle's® learn how important it is to keep their dog safe. This isn't just safe physically, but safe emotionally as well. Dogs experience emotions just like we do; fear, stress, anxiety, and trust. Not all dogs can handle every situation. Just like humans, there are some situations that you may be okay with, while others put you over the edge emotionally speaking. "Listen" to what your dog is saying and protect him. Doing so will allow your relationship to grow. Trust is the foundation of great training.

What should you do if a loose dog runs up to you? Or maybe even an out of control dog that makes you feel uncomfortable? I am apart of Doggone Safe's program called Be a Tree. We teach adults and children how to use their body in a way that makes you boring and encourages the dog to walk away. You will

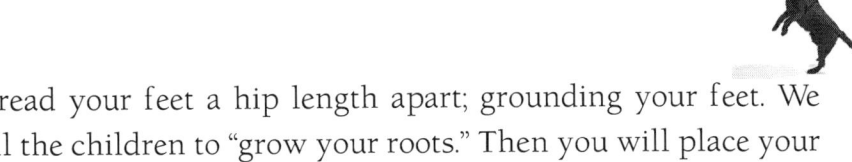

spread your feet a hip length apart; grounding your feet. We tell the children to "grow your roots." Then you will place your "branches" your arms resting in front of you interlocking your fingers. Then you will look down at your feet and count in your head as high as you can go.

Several months ago I volunteered for a 4th grade class to learn the Be a Tree program. Around a month later I had visited a family for an in-home training session and the mother shared her son came inside and shared with his mom that a pit pull ran up to him in the street and he said that he became like a tree and the dog walked away.

If you are interested in learning more about the Be a Tree program you can visit, www.doggonesafe.com. For more information on pregnancy and children interaction with dogs please visit, www.familypaws.com.

Children and Dogs

If you are a parent, grandparent, aunt, or babysitter, it is important that when children are interacting with a dog (no matter what age) that the adult is actively supervising. If the adult is unable to be actively supervising interaction then management is needed. Passive supervision is an adult in the room on computer, or the checking phone. Management would involve putting the dog in the kennel, another room, or outside. Why is this important? It is important to help children know appropriate interaction with dogs. This would include; how to pet, not to climb on the dog, or allow children to run around screaming. It is important that the adult is "listening" to what the dog is communicating and removing him from a situation that involves stress or him being uncomfortable. Creating a positive experience by using active supervision will also be a positive experience for the dog, the child, and also work towards being proactive in dog bite prevention.

Another situation that I had never really considered until I became a mother myself is, when my child visits a friend's home, aunt's home, grandparent's home are there dogs? It is important to have a dialogue about dogs with your children so they know not to interact with unknown dogs and also dialogue with the parents about active supervision and management.

Dog Bite Victims

If you have been a survivor of a dog bite, you know firsthand how traumatic this can be. For others, please know that being bit by a dog is very traumatic for both adults and children. If you have been a survivor of a dog bite or know of someone it is important that you seek counseling. Also www.doggonesafe. com has a dog bite victim support.

The Tapping Solution

Another amazing healing technique that can be used on animals and humans is , "The Tapping Solution" I was introduced to Nick and Jessica Ortner through their Tapping Summit. It changed my life and helped me to be an even better animal communicator and dog trainer.

This feature-length film explores E.F.T. or "Tapping", a new discovery that combines ancient Chinese acupressure and modern psychology,with startling results. The Tapping Solu-

tion explores Tapping in a way that's never been seen before. The film combines the wisdom and experience of world famous teachers, speakers, and motivators, with an element that's usually missing: REAL LIFE CASES, unfolding before your eyes. Ten people spend four days working with Tapping practitioners to see if they can turn their lives around. The results are fully documented and the ride is one you'll never forget. You can learn all about Nick and Jessica at www.thetappingsolution.com It is a fascinating way to heal.

Millions of people are settling for lives filled with poor health and emotional baggage. Not knowing how to achieve the joyful and satisfying lives they desire, they're stuck accepting a lifestyle of emotional trauma, chronic physical pain, compulsions and addictions, or perhaps just an empty feeling inside. Along with these problems come pills to kill the pain, sleep at night, and suppress anxiety – but this is hardly better than the disease.

If you're like many people, you feel trapped, caught in this cycle. You're tired of feeling sad, depressed, anxious, discontent, and unwell. You're sick of the expensive and ineffective treatments. You're fed up with relinquishing the power over your health and happiness to psychologists and doctors. You'd like to grow, flourish, and thrive, putting the past in the past. You want to be your best, living a life that is filled with peacefulness, joy, and fulfillment, from day to day and moment to moment.

With Tapping, you can do that. You can discover the vital secret for emotional wholeness and physical relief. You can take your physical and emotional well-being into your own hands. It's simple for anyone to master, and it's free.

Tapping provides relief from chronic pain, emotional problems, disorders, addictions, phobias, post traumatic stress disorder, and physical diseases. While Tapping is newly set to revolutionize the field of health and wellness, the healing concepts that it's based upon have been in practice in Eastern medicine for over 5,000 years. Like acupuncture and acupressure, Tapping is a set of techniques which utilize the body's energy meridian points. You can stimulate these meridian points by tapping on them with your fingertips – literally tapping into your body's own energy and healing power.

Your body is more powerful than you can imagine... filled with life, energy, and a compelling ability for self-healing. With Tapping, you can take control of that power.

So How Does It All Work?

All negative emotions are felt through a disruption of the body's energy. And physical pain and disease are intricately connected to negative emotions. Health problems create feedback – physical symptoms cause emotional distress, and unresolved emotional problems manifest themselves through physical symptoms. So, the body's health must be approached as a whole. You cannot treat the symptoms without addressing the cause, and vice-versa.

The body, like everything in the universe, is composed of energy. Restore balance to the body's energy, and you will mend the negative emotions and physical symptoms that stem from the energy disruption. Tapping restores the body's energy balance, and negative emotions are conquered.

The basic technique requires you to focus on the negative emotion at hand: a fear or anxiety, a bad memory, an unresolved problem, or anything that's bothering you. While maintaining your mental focus on this issue, use your fingertips to tap 5-7 times each on 12 of the body's meridian points. Tapping on these meridian points – while concentrating on accepting and resolving the negative emotion – will access your body's energy, restoring it to a balanced state.

You may be wondering about these meridians. Put simply, energy circulates through your body along a specific network of channels. You can tap into this energy at any point along the system.

This concept comes from the doctrines of traditional Chinese medicine, which referred to the body's energy as "ch'i." In ancient times, the Chinese discovered 100 meridian points. They also discovered that by stimulating these meridian points, they could heal. Call it energy, call it the Source, call it life force, call it ch'i... Whatever you want to call it, it works.

In some ways, Tapping is similar to acupuncture. Like Tapping, acupuncture achieves healing through stimulating the body's meridians and energy flow. However, unlike Tapping, acupuncture involves needles! "No needles" is definitely one of the advantages of Tapping.

Acupuncture also takes years to master. Acupuncture practitioners must memorize hundreds of meridian points along the body; the knowledge and training take years to acquire.

Tapping is simple and painless. It can be learned by anyone. And you can apply it to yourself, whenever you want, wherever you are. It's less expensive and less time consuming. It can be used with specific emotional intent towards your own unique life challenges and experiences. Most importantly, it gives you the power to heal yourself, putting control over your destiny back into your own hands.

I highly recommend you go to www.thetappingsolution.com to learn more and hear about the amazing work this talented brother and sister are doing together. I have seen incredible results in my own life and with clients I shared these techniques with have also been amazed at the wonderful benefits. I hope you will open your mind and give it a try.

Lessons learned in Chapter 3

1. Cultivate Positive emotions. Imagine you already have what you are hoping for take time to journal how that would make you feel?

   _____

   _____

   _____

   _____

   _____

2. Redirect negative self-talk into positive statements and write 5 affirmations to turn the negative ones around.

   _____

   _____

   _____

   _____

   _____

3. Feel gratitude for all the blessings in your life. Take time to write down 5 things that you are grateful for?

   _____

   _____

   _____

   _____

   _____

4. Focus only on what you want and don't place any focus on what you do not want to happen. Write here what you are hoping for and let the happy feelings of receiving them flow.

_____

_____

_____

_____

_____

Chapter 4

HOW YOUR POSITIVE THINKING AFFECTS YOUR DOG

"All of the knowledge and the totality of all questions and all answers are contained in a dog."

Kafica

Positive Thinking

Engaging in positive thinking certainly makes life more pleasurable. One positive thought is likely to generate another, creating a cycle. The steady stream of thoughts will flow, whether you direct it or not. Positive thinking and goal setting are now considered scientifically viable methods for changing a person's life.

> **Watch your thoughts, for they become words. Choose your words, for they become actions. Understand your actions, for they become habits. Study your habits, for they become your character. Develop your character, for it becomes your destiny.**
>
> **Anonymous**

Using positive thinking is a great way to get results. There is another great way you can communicate with your pets, it is called telepathy. Telepathy is the transference of thoughts, feelings, or images between two or more subjects.

An article in "The Huffington Post" asks the question; can your dog read your mind?

That was the question posed in a recent study published in the journal *Learning and Behavior* about canine behavior. The answer, apparently, is both a little bit yes and also, a little bit no.

Researchers at the University of Florida set out to better understand the origins of exactly how it is that dogs respond to human gestures, focusing specifically on what the study's lead author, Monique Udell, called "attentional states."

To do that, they set up several different experiments. Dogs from both domesticated situations and shelters were given the choice to beg for food from a person with her face or eyes concealed, versus one whose attention was fixed on the dogs. The same experiments were also conducted with wolves -- the idea being that it would show whether or not they have some kind of genetic barrier that prevents them from responding to cues of attention in the same way dogs can, as previous studies have suggested.

What the researchers found is that both the dogs and the wolves were less likely to beg for food from the experimenters who had their backs to them, which indicates a "capacity to behave in accordance with a human's attentional state," the authors wrote. In other words, most of the canines and wolves displayed some kind of ability -- perhaps inherent -- to sense how people were acting, regardless of whether or not they grew up in contact with humans.

But the researchers also found that, generally speaking, dogs raised as pet rather than in shelters were more likely to respond to cues when they had a human's attention. This indicates that in the course of living with, and being cared for by humans, they'd learned to better understand their cues.

"What this shows is that it's not a question of nature versus nurture," explained Udell. "It's always going to be a combination to the two that informs a dog's responsiveness to humans."

In other words, Fido does have some natural ability to sense when he's got your attention, but he hones that sense through a lifetime of experience, too.

Udell added that, people could take this information and use it to help train the dog of their dreams.

"Dogs aren't born being man's best friend," she said. "The experiences they have and the type of environment they live in -- these influence their behavior. If you want a dog that's very responsive to humans, that does take work."

Two Interviews with animal communicators

Animal Communicator: Animals communicate regularly through telepathy. It is the most basic form of communication, an ability we are all born with. As humans, we learn to rely on verbal communication and our telepathic skills are pushed aside and become rusty. Like a muscle, unless used regularly, these skills become weak and inefficient. Humans, given the proper mindset and training, have the ability to communicate telepathically with all species.

I am so excited to share two of my fellow animal communicators that are joining me in being a voice for the animals. This is Debbie McGillivray, the co-author of "Untamed Voices" she is an incredibly gifted animal communicator. You can find her at www.animaltelepathy.com **Communicating with an animal is a two way process, there is a sender and a receiver. Now here is the amazing part....telepathy can be done in person or over distance! A great example of this is when you are thinking of someone and the phone rings, lo and behold it is the very person you were just thinking about. Coincidence or Telepathy! We have all had telepathic experiences; we just don't recognize them as such.** Debby and I both believe that anyone can be telepathic; she suggests we do three simple things to begin.

1. Believe in yourself and your gifts.
2. Don't try too hard just allow yourself to be open to receiving anything.
3. Be still, and in the moment. In the moment is when miracles will happen.

My friend, Meredith Whitney, is also an amazing animal communicator of www.connectionswithcritters.com she describes how she connects with animals in her own words "spirit to spirit or heart to heart". She explains she receives visions and images. She truly believes that anyone can learn this teachable skill and shares her wisdom with Girl Scouts and 4H Groups. Children are more open to the possibility to communicate with animals. Many are extremely gifted and we want to cultivate this in children. It is very important that we begin to see the amazing possibilities for our planet if humans begin to understand the lessons animals are teaching. For just one moment; imagine a planet where every human believed their purpose was to be unconditional, forgiving, mindful, and joyful. We would transform the planet and this is what we the animal communicators know the animals are here to teach us. There is a beautiful meditation recorded on my website and you also have free access to the e-workbook to try some of these amazing exercises and techniques. Please have an open mind and heart as you explore and expand your spiritual gifts. It is my intention to be fully present for you, if you have any questions you can click on the contact me link on my website and I will answer you.

Lessons learned in Chapter 4

POSITIVE THINKING
5 Steps to stop a negative belief.

5 Steps to Dispel A limiting Belief ...
And Change your BRAIN Literally.

First: RECOGNIZE that it is a neural pattern that has nothing to do with the present moment.

Second: understand that your brain boils down information into «sound bites» that over-generalizes and oversimplifies the topic or issue.

Third: Identify your deepest most treasured CORE VALUES and then see if they support your old beliefs.

Fourth: RELEASE your old belief by observing it without judgment. It's just a memory tied to old images, feelings, and thoughts.

Fifth: REFRAME it. Create a new belief based on your core value. Then RETRAIN your brain by repeating your core value and new belief like a mantra.

Do this for about 10 minutes a day, and in less than eight weeks, brain researchers Newberg and Waldman's brain scan studies show that *your brain will actually change.*

Chapter 5

Awaken the Powerful Energy Centers in you and in your Pet

(Energy Healing)

Reiki

Definition

Reiki is a form of therapy that uses simple hands-on, no-touch, and visualization techniques, with the goal of improving the flow of life energy in a person. Reiki (pronounced *ray-key*) means "universal life energy" in Japanese, and Reiki practitioners are trained to detect and alleviate problems of energy flow on the physical, emotional, and spiritual level. Reiki touch therapy is used in the same way to achieve similar effects that traditional massage therapy is used—to relieve stress and pain, and to improve the symptoms of various health conditions.

Purpose

Reiki claims to provide many of the same benefits as traditional massage therapy, such as reducing stress, stimulating the immune system, increasing energy, and relieving the pain and symptoms of health conditions. Practitioners have reported success in helping patients with acute and chronic illnesses, from asthma and arthritis to trauma and recovery from surgery. Reiki is a gentle and safe technique, and has been used successfully in some hospitals. It has been found to be very calming and reassuring for those suffering from severe or fatal conditions. Reiki can be used by doctors, nurses, psychologists and other health professionals to bring touch and deeper caring into their healing practices.

Reiki on animals is a very soothing and effective way to help your pet. We have seven main energy centers in our body. There are seven primary chakras, or energy centers sometimes called wheels, that flow through the body along the spinal cord. The chakra energy system lies within more than just the physical state of being. Each charka is correlated with different aspects of our lives.

Rei means "spirit," and Ki means "energy," so literally, the word Reiki translates as "spiritual energy." Thus in reality, all things consist of Reiki, since all things are made of energy. This energy travels through us to the beings who need healing. We often feel it more strongly as coming through our hands, but in reality Reiki flows through all our energy centers and pathways (i.e. chakras and meridians), so is moving throughout our whole body. The more you practice with Reiki, the more you will feel the energy flow.

Reiki is also used to describe a Japanese energy healing system used originally for spiritual development and used today for "hands-on" healing. We are called "practitioners" of this system not "healers" since we are not actually manipulating energy for healing; rather we are creating an energetic space to support the self-healing process of the being to whom we are connecting. In reality, each individual is responsible for his or her own healing process, and Reiki is a way to support this.

The system of Reiki is defined as a "practice," so your intention and commitment to the "doing" of Reiki is important to your development, healing, and understanding of the healing process, as well as your ability to access a deeper energetic space. Doing Reiki can deepen your intuition and cause tremendous internal healing on all levels. It is also holistic: it can be used for physical, mental/emotional, and spiritual healing. As the nature of Reiki supports energetic balance and harmony, it always finds the origin of the problem (since all health problems are "dis-ease" or imbalance) and works for the highest good (rebalancing and clearing the energy "flow").

Reiki is ideal for use with animals because it is gentle, non-invasive and doesn't require physical contact. It doesn't cause stress, discomfort, or pain, and yet yields powerful results. Animals respond intuitively to Reiki's power to support the healing of emotional, behavioral, and physical illnesses and injuries.

For animals who are healthy, Reiki helps to maintain their health, enhances relaxation and provides an emotional sense of peace and contentment.

For animals who are ill, Reiki is a wonderful healing method as well as a safe complement to Western Medicine, Chinese Medicine, homeopathy, flower essences, and all other forms of healing. For example, Reiki can reduce the side effects of chemotherapy, support an acupuncture treatment, and complement the effects of flower essences.

For dying animals, Reiki is a powerful yet gentle way to provide comfort, relief from pain, fear, and anxiety, and to ease the transition to death. Reiki is also a wonderful way to support a dying animal's family.

- 1st Chakra- Muladhara- root located at the base of the spine
- 2nd Chakra- Svadhisthana- sacral located a few inches above the root chakra
- 3rd Chakra- Manipura- power or solar flexes located just above the belly button
- 4th Chakra- Anahata- love is located at the heart
- 5th Chakra- Vishuddha- communication is located on the throat
- 6th Chakra- Ajna- intuition (third eye) is located between the eyebrows
- 7th Chakra Sahasrara-(crown) divine is located on the top of the head.

Colors for Chakras

1. Root — Red
2. Sacral — Orange
3. Solar plexes — yellow
4. Heart — Green
5. Throat — Blue
6. Between the eyes — Indigo
7. Top of head — Violet

I will be doing demonstrations on my website and you will have activities in your workbook. I suggest you apply all of what you have learned so far in this book and set the intention that you are a wonderful Reiki Master. Please enjoy all of these exercises as if it were a science experiment. Let go of all doubts. Trust your inner guidance that I have spoken about in prior meditations. Have fun with this process it is a great adventure and you will experience much more fulfilling relationships. I am your guide so if you have any questions please reach out to me I will reach back. This is OUR divine assignment.

Meditation of Reiki

Just for Today
I will not anger

Just for Today
I will not worry

Just for Today
I will do my work honestly

Just for Today
I will be kind to all living things

Just for Today
I will give thanks for my many blessings

Lessons Learned in Chapter five

Energy Healing

1. What are the seven energy centers and where are they located?
   _____
   _____
   _____
   _____
   _____

2. Name three ways to know when a chakra is blocked?
   _____
   _____
   _____
   _____
   _____

3. What are the colors of each chakra?
   _____
   _____
   _____
   _____
   _____

Chapter 6

THIS ALL SOUNDS GREAT BUT I WANT TO SEE SOME RESULTS

Karma and Paco

"Everything in life comes to you as a teacher pay attention and you will learn quickly."

Cherokee Saying

I n this chapter I will share true stories of lives transformed. These are my clients who have become my spirit family. You will notice how the principles I teach spill over into many areas of their lives and have improved their relationships. I am very grateful to do God's work and to help people and pets. I know this is my higher purpose. I will be going into elementary schools and teaching children the benefits of environmental education, animal advocacy, and mindfulness. I truly feel it is the missing link; children need to have kindness cultivated in them. I really believe this will transform the planet. Please join me in this mission by signing up at my website to receive a monthly newsletter. It will be filled with inspirational true stories. We are all part of the solution. God has made that perfectly clear and I am honored to be a voice for all animals and children. They are our messengers of hope.

These are interviews with my clients. I have been working with them for years and the results have been amazing to all of us. That is why I decided to write this book, I know that anyone can achieve these results if they apply simple principles to their practice. I choose to be with you every step of the way and I envision a day when all my readers will connect with me. I hope this resonates with your heart and you can open your mind to the possibilities. My clients have all been thrilled for years and have continued these practices. They refer people to me all the time; my business has grown from word of mouth which to me is the greatest compliment.

Bella

My first client is Vicky; I have been working for her for three years. We have been through many challenges and have connected and helped each other in many ways. Vicky is the owner of two beautiful dogs ,a few months ago she lost one of her dogs to kidney failure. Vicky was very comforted by my gift because I was able to relay messages from her departed dog. This brought her a sense of peace she still had one dog, a beautiful Dalmatian named Bella.

Vicky rescued Bella; Bella had severe anxiety from the abuse she endured before Vicky adopted her. Bella was extremely afraid of everything. Vicky has arthritis and other difficult health issues. She was unable to walk Bella. She hired me and here is what she has to say about the work we have done together. Vicky says, "Karen, you have worked miracles; she is a completely different dog. She used to be afraid to go out of the house. She was afraid and barked uncontrollably in the house. She jumped on company and being a big dog she intimidated people. Within a few weeks of working with you, she looks forward to her walks. She does not bark or jump on people anymore. She is a confident and well-behaved dog."

Vicky also shared how difficult it was to adopt another dog. She was depressed from losing her dog but wanted to get another dog. She began to apply the law of attraction principles and she found the perfect dog to adopt. Her name is Brandy; she is a smaller dog and Bella loved her immediately. Brandy came with her own set of issues. She struggled with abandonment and was extremely fearful of strangers. Brandy was left on the streets of a busy city and she was pregnant. A wonderful rescue organization found her and took great care of her. She lost all her puppies and was very malnourished. When Vicky saw her it was love at first sight and she knew her prayers had been answered. She asked me to work with this little darling and within a week she let go of all her fears. She loves going for walks and playing with other dogs. She is very well-behaved and extremely smart. She loves the training and enjoys the attention. She lives in the moment, so she is a very happy and content dog. I wonder why it takes us humans so long to get this lesson.

Vicky also feels the law of attraction, Reiki, and mindfulness has helped her health and also the injury that Bella had. I have been sharing these gifts with Vicky and her dogs; she feels it has spilled over into her life and her health and emotional issues have been healing. Vicky now believes that positive thinking has helped her with her pain. She feels that Brandy and Bella are healers; they fill her days with so much joy and happiness. She also feels that my energy helps the dogs to be more peaceful. The most touching part of this interview was when Vicky told me I have a gift that is very special. She believes I am an animal communicator and spiritual medium. She feels the techniques have helped her and that I have helped change her life for the better. She told me our relationship has helped her with her own faith. I feel so blessed to work with people and pets, to help them discover the magic inside them. I believe that God guides me and I listen. Vicky is part of my family; she has empowered me to speak the truth and to trust in my amazing gifts. I am extremely grateful to God that guided us to each other's lives.

Sam

An Interview with Cindy

Cindy and I have been friends for years. We both had old dogs at the same time and we comforted each other when they passed on.

Cindy shared a beautiful letter about Charley and Sam.

Cindy's comments:

"There is nothing worse in life than to lose a loved one, whether it is a two-legged human, or a four-legged pet. The pain from losing my beloved Charley was overwhelming.

'I always knew that someday, I would lose Charley, but I would put it out of my mind, thank God that I had him for 1 year, for 2 years, for 3 years, and so on. Until the dreaded day that my husband and I had to make the split-second decision to give Charley the gift of everlasting life and to end his suffering.

'That day, I will never forget, was 10-10-10. I miss him dearly. I treasure all of the wonderful times that we had together. I remember every detail about him. He was certainly not perfect physically; but he was beautiful to me.

I had so much love in my heart to give. I was walking with my girlfriend one day and she told me she saw an ad for yellow lab puppies. She told me about the ad because she knew I had been searching and searching the local humane societies and pet rescue organizations for a yellow lab; only to be disappointed because as soon as one came in, it was adopted immediately.

'I ended up having the pick of the litter and chose my little Sam. His full name is Sampson, named after the biblical character. With the wonderful and expert help from Karen, Sam has truly become the strong and confident Sampson. He is full of love.

'His love radiates out, and I attribute that to Karen's personality and guidance. When Sam got sick and was in the hospital for a week, when he saw Karen on her visits, even though he could not eat or drink, he managed a weak tail wag for her, his beloved Karen. It was her prayers and powerful positive energy called Reiki that helped bring him back to life, I truly believe it.

'To this day, Sam loves and holds Karen near and dear to his heart.

'If anyone loses a pet, and thinks that they cannot go through the heartache of adopting another one and loving it for years, only to lose it again, think about this: you have so much love to give, and to share. It doesn't stop when our pet dies; it grows and grows inside of you and is ready to burst out of your heart as a testament to the love that you had for your pet that just passed away.

'It took me 8 months to come to grips with losing Charley. You never get over losing your beloved pet, you just learn how to live with the grief, because the grief slowly *gives way to a softer pain, then a distant pain, then a quiet comfort, and then finally, love.*

"It is this love that you will find that you want to share with another pet, and it will be that much stronger because you have loved and lost, and know what is in store the next time around."

Cindy decided to get a puppy, when she was ready she adopted a beautiful yellow lab puppy. Cindy asked me to train Sam when he turned 4 months old. I always tell people this is the ideal time to start training; and it was. Sam did have a few issues but I was able to help him step into his greatness. He comes with me everywhere, he is extremely social and I have been blessed to work with him for two years. Applying these techniques has helped him with his fears and I always help him conquer his fears so they never grew into phobias.

Cindy feels more confident in her skills and says she learned very quickly and stays consistent with his training. She says it has improved her relationship with her husband too. She uses it at work and with any stressful situations. Cindy shared with me that learning the law of attraction has helped her life on many levels. She has applied these skills in all areas of her life and says she has complete peace of mind. She says that she knows my gifts are from God because of the way dogs react to me. There is a divine connection that anyone can see. She tells me that Sam knows when I will be coming and waits by the gate. Sam and I are telepathic with each other and I am very grateful.

My friendship with Cindy is a confirmation that God's love guided me to this family. I cherish my relationship with Cindy;

she helped me believe in myself. She is a big part of why I am writing this book. My gifts have made people feel comfortable; Cindy was always encouraging. We have been a gift to each other and I know that God led us to each other.

My friends and clients, Pamela and David, with their beautiful dogs

Karma and Paco

I decided to take a business class to help expand my non-profit organization. The class was amazing and I loved my teacher and all my classmates. I was learning all the nuts and bolts of how to run a small business. I felt so empowered and excited and learned to speak in front of audiences; a huge fear of mine.

I conquered each defeating thought and completed the assignments. My teacher was such an inspiration. She is a successful woman, business owner and she presented herself with such confidence and poise. I thought to myself, *someday that will be me.*

I was getting very close to all my classmates. Each week, we wrote down one of our talents we would like to share with our class. I shared my pet care business and my classmate David asked me if I could walk his two dogs. He invited me to his house but warned me that his dog, Karma, was extremely afraid of strangers.

I prayed to God to help me bond with Karma and asked God to help me connect and communicate with her. I was reminded that I used to have trust issues and God was bringing us together to help each other. It was not an accident. David was amazed how quickly Karma and I bonded. He said, "Wow, she never lets any stranger put a leash on her." I could feel God's love flowing through the leash.

Paco

Paco was David's second dog; he was a ball of fun and energy. Paco is a beautiful ridgeback. He benefitted from my calm peaceful energy too. I still remember our first walk together. I calmed him and taught him not to jump on people.

I felt Karma saying, "I trust you so please don't hurt me, I have trusted humans and they have hurt me." I felt tears welling up in my eyes as she snuggled in close to me.

I said, "I promise I will never hurt you and you can feel safe with me, I will protect you." She became more confident around strangers and little by little began to trust.

David and Pam took a trip to Montana and they hired

a couple to house sit and stay with the dogs. I got a call from them in Montana, asking me to go over and help because Karma would not let the people touch her. I went over and explained to Karma that her people would be back soon but for now this was her pack. I promised her they will be very good to her.

The people were very sweet and patient and Karma let them touch her. I gave them a brush she loves and they brushed her. She let them put her leash on and the two weeks went by fast. I checked on everyone twice a week and the pups were very happy.

When David and Pam returned home I knew this was an-other confirmation I really was telepathically communicating with Karma. Pam mentioned she never saw Karma so calm and content.

I asked God to guide me to where I could be most helpful just like I learned in "The Course in Miracles." Miracles were happen-ing everywhere I went. . I am so grateful and God continues to give me more beautiful gifts.

Lacy; a happy dog

My good friend called me she was very excited because she adopted a beautiful golden retriever. My friend Gail was very excited and happy to have a new member to the family. She lost her dog Katie to cancer a few months ago. Lacy was a dream come true for Gail and her husband Randy. Gail explained to me that Lacy was very nervous and reserved around strangers. She also suffered from separation anxiety and could not be left alone. I was hired to stay with Lacy while Gail ran some errands. When I arrived Lacy was distant, she was very nervous but calmed down as I began to use some calming techniques with her. I was able to connect with Lacy and communicate with her. She let me know she had a nice family and one day they just left her on the street. She wanted to believe that her new family with Gail and Randy would be wonderful but she had major trust issues. I help my hand to her heart and telepathically communicated to her that she could believe in us. I promised her this would be her forever home and her new family loved her. She lit up and I began working with her once a week. Gail said, " I don't know what you have done but she is a different dog, she is just the best dog. " I used the techniques I have shared throughout this book and you will see in the pictures she smiles when I come to work with her. She loves her training and socializing time. This dog had fear and anxiety because she was abandoned. I was able to work with her and within a few weeks I earned her trust and respect. Then I helped Gail to communicate and connect with her and the love that Gail and Randy have for Lacy is a true happy ending for a dog that did not have the best beginning.

Darby; a dog who was left to die

My dear friend C.C called me she is the owner and founder of www.happyendingsanimalrescuesanctuary.org ; an incredible animal rescue organization where I volunteer. I help dogs with intense behavior issues heal their issues and become the amazing dogs they truly are. My friend called me because she saved the life of a dog named Darby. He spent his life being used as dog bait in dog fighting. He was muzzled and attacked to build up the dogs that were fighting. He was left to die, tied to a tree with no food or water for six days. One of the neighbors contacted C.C. and she went to rescue him. She saved his life got him to her vet and he survived but was very aggressive. C.C. called me and asked me to start to work with Darby. I meditated and prayed; asking to be helpful to this beautiful dog. He is a Catahoula and Australian Sheppard. I knew God was leading me to help this amazing dog. The first moment we met there was an incredible connection. He looked at me so deeply I could feel he knew I was there to help. I prayed and felt guided to do some Reiki and energy work with him. I placed my hand on his heart and I felt all his pain and saw visions of the horrible abuse he endured. Tears filled my eyes as I remembered the abuse I had suffered through all those years ago. It was the most magical moment of pure love and we developed a mutual trust and respect like it had never felt before. I loved working with Darby; he is such a smart dog and really wants to please. In one week he was doing awesome, I was teaching him how to play ball and he loved going for rides in my truck. I took him to the park and started to introduce him to strangers. He completely trusts me and loves to meet new people. He knows I will never hurt him or bring him to any danger. He is really doing great but needs to find a program that offers rehabilitation with other dogs. I am starting a blog and facebook page for Darby to give him the best chance. The sanctuary is a wonderful place but he really needs to be able to run and get lots of exercise and he needs help with socializing. He is very loved at the sanctuary and enjoys the attention and great care he receives. Darby has confirmed for me again that dogs are unconditional, forgiving, they live in the moment, and just spread joy. I have learned so much working with these phenomenal animals.

Lessons from Bella, Brandy, Darby, Lacy, Karma, Paco and Sam

1. Treat dogs and people with trust and respect and they will treat you the same.

2. Believe in yourself and always do your best; then expect miracles to happen and they will.

3. Show gratitude for all the blessings in your life and blessing will appear everywhere.

4. Become present, stay focused on the moment, with every task and infuse it with love. Love what you do and do one thing at a time.

5. Have patience and let go of any judgment. Then step back and watch what happens.

Chapter 7

MINDFULNESS
WILL IMPROVE YOUR LIFE

"Faith means living with uncertainty, feeling your way through life, letting your heart guide you like a lantern in the dark."

Dan Millman

An Interview with a Mindful Expert, my friend

ANN WHITE has lived many lives in this one earthly lifetime

Corporate problem solver and trainer for Fortune 500 companies
Board Certified Marital and Family Attorney specializing in
domestic violence and divorce
Rabbi
Trauma Chaplain
Grief Counselor

Transformational Author
The Sacred Art of Dog Walking,
Making the Ordinary Extraordinary
Living with Spirit Energy,
Bring Balance and Harmony into Your Life and World
Pebbles in the Pond,
Transforming the World One Person at a Time

You can find Ann at www.creatingcalmwithinchaos.com in our interview she describes being mindful as being fully present as life unfolds. She encourages people to stay conscious and truly observe nature. This is considered mindful walking. I encourage you to try this exercise with your dog on your next walk.

Mindful walking is one way to promote mindfulness skills without having to make time for formal practice. Try this simple exercise to promote mindful walking, inspired by Thich Nhat Hahn's book *Peace Is Every Step: The Path of Mindfulness in Everyday Life* (Bantam, 1992), which provides lots of examples of ways to incorporate mindfulness practice into activities you already engage in every day.

Here's How:

If at any point during your walk you notice your mind is wandering to the past or the future, or being pulled away from the walk, just gently acknowledge that your mind has wandered and bring yourself back to the present moment and the walk. Remember that being pulled away and coming back is the key to mindfulness practices, no one has perfect focus. Remember each step you have arrived. Feel the present moment and embrace it with your breath and awareness.

Ann explains that animals are divine because as it says in the bible, God gave animals the breath of life. Dogs are always teaching humans to be present and live in the moment. They use all their senses in each experience. Humans are too busy to get from point A to point B, we miss the opportunities to be fully present. This is the GIFT our dogs want to give us.

Ann shared that becoming mindful changed her life. She has stopped living in a state of worry, panic, and fear because she lets life unfold without judging she has deep inner peace. She shares this in her wonderful book, "The Sacred Art of Dog walking".

A Miracle Blesses Everyone

This is a true story that Ann shared with me. This story confirmed to me that animals are telepathic and emotional. They want to connect with us on a deeper level and are talking to us, if we will listen. Ann did listen and she was able to help a beautiful family. She is a Trauma Chaplain and a Rabbi; she was visiting a man who was on his death bed. The man was dying and he was peaceful and ready to leave his body but his dog was very upset. Ann asked if she could have a few moments alone with the pup. The man's wife was very grateful and said yes. Ann connected with this little dog telepathically. She sent a picture to the dog that his owner was going to die. She explained to the dog; he would be okay. She sent a message that his new job would be to help the wife. The dog was very grateful and so was the man. The little dog jumped up on the bed gave the man a kiss and the man passed peacefully knowing his dog would be cared for.

Benefits of Mindfulness

Being mindful literally lowers your stress level. Health Psychologist says mindfulness decreases levels of the stress hormone cortisol.

Mindfulness makes people more compassionate according to a study done in "The Journal of Psychological Science".

Decreases feelings of depression; research from the University Of California, Los Angeles found that applying mindfulness helped decreases loneliness among the elderly and boosted their health.

Lowered depression risk in teens according to a study from University of Leuven, the practice of mindfulness could help teens experience less stress, anxiety, and depression.

According to a survey of psychologists conducted by Consumer's Report, mindfulness training was considered an excellent strategy for weight loss. The mindful walks you take with your dog will benefit you and your dog.

The University of Utah's study found that mindfulness training helps control our emotions and moods. It also helps us sleep better.

I will be sharing on my blog and in my videos many techniques that will help you in your practice of mindfulness. I hope you will give it a try and you will see the benefits for yourself. I became a yoga instructor because yoga saved my life. I have learned to use the practice of mindfulness in everything I do. I observe and do not judge. It has helped me in all areas of my life and I know it will help you too. I am dedicated to your success. I truly believe in you and I am here to be truly helpful.

Lessons learned from Chapter 7

MINDFULNESS

1. Can you spend five minutes a day just observing your thoughts? Please have no opinion or judgements. List 5 things that came up for you?

    _____

    _____

    _____

    _____

    _____

2. When you are practicing your mindful walk with your dog please share here what thoughts, feelings, and emotions are coming up for you?

    _____

    _____

    _____

    _____

    _____

3. Practice eating mindfully take each bite and chew for 30 times. Savor the flavors, pay attention to the smells, and texture. Try to use all five senses and make it a truly

enjoyable experience. Make sure to always eat before your dog and establish that this is a calm time of the day. Do not serve your dog when it is in an excited state of mind. Share here what you notice about this new practice.

_____

_____

_____

_____

_____

Chapter 8

WHAT YOUR DREAMS ARE TRYING TO TEACH YOU

*Kelly Sullivan Walden says dreams have a language
all their own—and being fluent in that language
reveals the wisdom to live the life of your dreams
while you're awake.*

Author, certified clinical hypnotherapist, inspirational speaker and founder of *Dream-Life Coach Training*, Kelly hosts a weekly web-radio show *The D-Spot*, is featured Dream Expert for *Fox News*, and recently appeared on the *Ricki Lake* Show. She has written seven books including the Amazon.com #1 bestseller *I Had The Strangest Dream*, as well as articles published in *Woman's World*, *Cosmopolitan*, *Seventeen*, and the Los Angeles Times.

Are dreams of departed loved ones simply memories playing out in the dreamscape, helping the bereaved to move through the grieving process? Or are our beloved departed's dream visitations actual encounters? You can find more information about Kelly and her books at www.kellywaldensullivan.com

I believe they can certainly be both. However, according to Elisabeth Kübler-Ross, dreams about our loved ones on the other side of the veil are "true contacts on a spiritual plane with messages for the living."

You may be surprised to discover that you might also have a message to deliver to the departed. Think of the communication as a two-way street that can allow for resolution and/or the fulfillment of a soul contract. Ultimately, these dreams are a gift to not only help you stay connected with those you love, but to give you direct access to your "super-natural" power, blessings, and the wisdom of your multi-dimensional soul.

Unless you are a lucid dreaming expert, it's difficult to press the dream button and ensure your loved one on the other side will come through in your dreams on demand when you say so. However, I believe that we can do our part, and then let them meet us the rest of the way.

If you'd like to receive a dreamtime message from a beloved on the other side of the veil, I suggest the following: This can be for a beloved pet too that has passed on. "Love is Forever"

- *Light a candle*

- *Take a look at a photograph of the person, or hold an heirloom in your hands that you associate with them.*

- *Close your eyes, and envision an energizing memory of the person...perhaps your best memory.*

- *With eyes closed, or while gazing upon their photo in a meditative way, form a question you have for them. Or you can simply pose the intent, "Relay a message to me in the dreamtime regarding 'x'."*

The most important thing to know as you drift into dreamland is that your personal angels (aka your departed loved ones) are with you. Breathe in the fact that their wisdom and love is here for you any time you need or desire it. You can stop feeling alone in the world, for if you could fathom how much support and guidance there is beaming down upon you from the other side, you would never cry again. You are held in a supernatural web of light, miracles, and prayers. Let this energy and guidance inform your steps, words, and decisions. Tap into the higher view of your deceased loved ones to envision how they see you and the ways in which they are rooting for and assisting you.

> *"Though we appear to be sleeping, there is an inner wakefulness that directs the dream...that will eventually startle us back to the truth of who we are."*
>
> *Rumi*

When you nestle yourself into bed, turn off the bedside lamp, and close your eyes to your daytime reality, your "conscious self" goes to sleep. Meanwhile, your "dreaming self" slips out of the covers and tiptoes upstairs to the attic of your mind to explore the enchanted realm of dreams.

Within this nocturnal territory you are transported beyond the ego's five senses to a vast, multidimensional playground of unlimited possibilities. In the realm of dreams you can peruse the tale of your past or future; learn a topic of fascination; converse with a departed loved one; study at the feet of a master; find an answer to a perplexing question; discover the solutions to a health challenge; or explore the larger story of your life.

All of this takes place while you are "asleep." Yet for most people, by the time the alarm blares and the morning coffee is guzzled, the exploration of the vast landscape of their multidimensional soul is shrugged off as "just a dream." This "just a dream" scenario can be compared to spellbound lovers on a shipboard romance who profess undying love to one another by moonlight, and then find, in the harsh light of morning, back on dry land, the glow is gone. In the swirl of "real world" demands, the lovers revert to being ordinary, sensible, earthbound mortals, vaguely recalling that something magical transpired aboard the ocean of their dreams. The experience—so real while it was happening—is now elusive as wisps of cloud.

But, what if it wasn't "Just a dream?"

Many of us 21st Century, fast-paced jet-setters fall prey to placing undo emphasis on the tangible, the text-able, and the three-dimensional, while discounting the magical, the mystical, and the multidimensional. We would do well to learn from our ancestors who lived close to the earth and were in sync with the tides, seasons, and realms beyond the ordinary. Our indigenous grandmothers and grandfathers considered the dreamtime to be when they were most "awake." They also believed that a society's mental and psychological health was related to dreaming. The more disconnected from dreams, the more sick and out of balance the society. The more in touch with dreams, the healthier a society becomes.

Unfortunately, most people think...

- Dreams are unimportant

- They don't have time to record, share, and/or work with their dreams

- They've lost touch with their ability to remember their dreams

Consider the fact that...

- Science tells us we all dream 3-9 dreams every night and can re-learn to re-member our dreams

- Dreams (even the unpleasant ones) can become our greatest ally

We cannot afford *not* to pay attention to our dreams, if we want to thrive while being alive.

Kelly shared a true story that confirms that love is forever and we have a purpose here on Earth. Our purpose is to love and learn from each other; it does not matter what our outer circumstances look like, we are whole and complete.

The following is a story about how a 14-year old girl's night-time dreams continues to help her and her family access a higher level of awakening.

Bridge Angel

Here are a few true stories that Kelly shared with me during our interview.

Claire came to see me because she wanted support and confirmation regarding a puzzling series of dreams. When she entered my office, I saw a diminutive 14-year old girl (a miniature *Angelina Jolie meets Anne Hathaway*). In most regards, Claire is a beautiful, charming and vivacious... utterly typical of her age.

However, Claire is atypical in one important way: since infancy she has suffered from cystic fibrosis. "Suffered" is perhaps too harsh a word, since aside from the oxygen tank at her side and the tubes running into her nose, and the treatments that include having her lungs vibrated for an hour or two a day, you would scarcely see a difference between Claire and any other bright, precocious, teenage girl.

Being in and out of the hospital is an ordinary part of Claire's life. A year before our meeting she was in a coma with a three percent chance of survival. Shortly after miraculously reviving from her coma, she had the following dream:

> My best friend, Alicia, and I are walking through a playground and we come across this twisted vine that catches our attention because it reminds us of "Jack and the Bean Stalk." When we touch the vine it carries us (like a turbo speed magic carpet) up to the "galaxy." We end up in a place high above the clouds. It is the most magical and beautiful place I've ever seen. Not only is it filled with the most brilliant colors, but it is also filled with the answers to every question we could think of. For example, Alicia has "boy problems," but up here in the galaxy, she completely understands why the boy she likes doesn't call or text her when he says he will—it all makes perfect sense!
>
> I asked a question I've always wanted to know the answer to: "Why do I have this illness?"
>
> The answer was revealed immediately.

"You've done good work in this life and in past lives. Your reward for all the light you have brought to others is the gift of a short life. You won't have to grow old like so many other people. You will get to have a lot of friends; bring joy to many people; make a difference in the world by shining light on CF (Cystic Fibrosis) through your foundation (Claire's Place), and then you get to leave, without having to grow old."

This answer makes me feel so good. I no longer have to think of my illness as a punishment for something I've done wrong or because I'm bad.

We explore the "galaxy" for what seems like months, having the best time ever. Up here I don't need my oxygen tank or my medical treatments at all!

At some point we realize we've been gone awhile and we don't want our families back on earth to worry about us so we travel back down the vine to earth. Luckily, in earth time, we were only gone a few minutes. Whew!

Back on earth we receive a letter telling us that we are "Bridge Angels" who have been given a special mission to find people who have just died and take them to the "galaxy." Most people don't know how to get there on their own so they need a Bridge Angel to escort them. Since we know how to get there, we are perfect for the job.

Alicia and I are so excited to have such an important assignment...especially because we know from personal experience how AMAZING this place is...we can't wait to share it with people!

I have this dream a lot, and so far we have taken hundreds of people to the "galaxy"— all kinds of people, young and old, every ethnicity and religion. They all die in different ways. From the human perspective it all seems so tragic, but when Alicia and I are in Bridge Angel mode, it isn't tragic at all. Even though every person we take to the galaxy loves it once they get there, at first they resist us, because they are afraid of leaving their familiar world and loved ones behind...and who could blame them.

We have to be very convincing. We found this out the hard way. Once there was a man so stubborn he wouldn't let us take him...so we finally let him go. We found out later that no one could find him because he had apparently gotten "lost." This made us realize the seriousness of our job. Since that moment we have never let another one slip by, no matter how much they kick and scream. In every case, each person we take to the "galaxy", once they see the beautiful colors and feel how wonderful it is to be there, they hug us, thank us for taking them, and walk into the light with a smile on their face.

Dreams Are Not Just for the Dreamer

Because Claire walks a fine line, in real life, between here and the hereafter, this dream has become a source of peace and reassurance for her and her family—especially her seven-year-old sister, Elly. Each time Claire gets hospitalized (which is frequent), little Elly gets scared and seeks reassurance from Claire. Claire and Elly share a bedroom and sometimes Elly asks Claire to tell her Bridge Angel bedtime stories. These stories reassure Elly and send her to dreamland with a smile on her face:

> *"Tell me again about the galaxy."*
>
> *"What is it like to be a Bridge Angel?"*
>
> *"When I die, will you be my Bridge Angel?"*
>
> *"Can I come visit you in the galaxy before I die, or do I have to wait 'til I die?"*
>
> *"Can we paint pictures of you in the galaxy so I know where you are going to be when you die?"*

Ancient dream cultures, such as the Senoi of Malaysia, believe that dreams are not only for the dreamer, but are meant to be shared so that the entire tribe may benefit. This is definitely the case for Claire's "Bridge Angel" dream. When I spoke with Claire's mother, Melissa, she told me that she, too, takes refuge in the dream.

> *"Claire's Dream has been a great gift to me. It gives me a strange comfort in the midst of what would otherwise be unthinkable emotional pain. In some way it seems this dream is preparing me (us)— like nothing else could—*

to cope with what would normally be an unbearable situation (having a child with special needs is frequently hospitalized, and the constant threat of impending death) by giving us a positive frame to put around it. One of the reasons for this odd feeling of peace we are able to hold onto is because Claire has embraced death in a powerful way. She is teaching us how to have a positive outlook on death, hers and our own. Because of her dream, Claire sees death and the afterlife as if it were a fabulous vacation she is preparing to take. She speaks of her dream locale in such vivid detail, we all share the mental imagery of this place, and it feels so real. There is comfort in knowing that if Claire gets there before us, we have a place to meet and be together again."

In the meantime, Claire is in no hurry to die...she is focused on living life to the fullest while she is here, and inspiring others to do the same. See for yourself by going to Claire's Facebook page: http://www.facebook.com/clairewineland and to her foundation: http://clairesplacefoundation.org. So far she's helped to organize three flash mobs, was a featured speaker at a recent TED conference, and had a NBC news special televised about her.

The most inspirational thing about Clair to me is when her mind wanders to thoughts of death or dying, a peaceful smile crosses her face...because her dream has revealed to her one of the greatest secrets, according to Native American Indians, *"To be unafraid of death...but to live fully, as if death were right over your shoulder."*

And who knows, maybe she really is a *Bridge Angel* who is actually helping transport newly departed souls to the other side during her dreamtime. All I know is when my time comes, there's no one but Claire I'd want to be my escort to the hereafter!

Kelly shares a beautiful story about how she connected with her beloved dog Woofie. Please begin to think about ways your loved ones who have passed are trying to connect with you. Spend time each night asking them to come close and your bond will never be broken. "

Soon after my beloved 14 year old dog, Woofie, passed away (on Valentine's Day 2012, I had the following dream:

> *I'm at a party where everyone is whining about something. I don't really want to be there, but I don't have the energy to leave—I'm feeling stuck. Suddenly my phone rings. It's my friend Cynthia Kersey (who, in real life wrote a book called 'Unstoppable'—this is an important detail.) She tells me to come to San Diego for her party. To entice me to drive the 2 hours from LA to San Diego she tells me I can have my very own 'Hamlet.' This shocks me—I'm not sure what a Hamlet is. Isn't it a village? At the very least I imagine it to be a quaint Germanic-styled condo in which to stay the night. This motivates me to leave from the party and begin making tracks to the 'Hamlet.'*

I awoke from that dream, wrote it down as I always do, and circled the word, *Hamlet*, because it seemed so bizarre; it caused my brow to furrow; and it stood out from the rest of the dream.

It seemed out of place from the rest of the dream. Not to mention even within the context of the dream it hooked my attention and had me switch directions from where I was planted. I couldn't figure out what 'Hamlet' meant (other than I'd been quite the melancholy damsel since my beloved Woofie passed away)...so I put it in the "unsolved mysteries" file.

The next day I went to my local nursery to buy a tree to plant for Woofie's memorial ceremony (yes...Woofie wasn't just a *dog* to me... she was family.)

> *It came to me that every time I lose a dog, they take a piece of my heart with them. And every new dog who comes into my life gifts me with a piece of their heart. If I live long enough, all the components of my heart will be dog, and I will become as generous and loving as they are.*
>
> *Unknown*

I told the sales clerk at the nursery what I was looking for (probably in a way that some would say was TMI—too much information—but I wanted her to help me get the right tree.)

"Excuse me," said a woman shopping behind me, "I didn't mean to eavesdrop on your conversation...but I just lost my dog a month ago and also looked for the right kind of tree or bush to plant to honor her. I planted rosemary because in the play *Hamlet* Ophelia hands Hamlet a sprig and tells him, *Rosemary is for remembrance.*"

My jaw drops to the ground. And then to drive the point home even further she shows me the locket she is wearing around her neck, containing a small photo of her Golden Retriever, and an engraving on the outside is an image of a sprig of rosemary, with the quote, 'Rosemary is for Remembrance.' Hamlet'

To that the sales clerk said, "We just received the most beautiful rosemary bush, it's right next to you."

It was love at first sight...this gorgeous 41/2-foot rosemary bush with tiny lilac-colored sprouts went home with me and stands gloriously in honor of Woofie, as well as for the remembrance of love and new life.

Besides leading me to find the perfect (burning) bush to plant for Woofie's memorial, this little dream wisp—that was out of character with the rest of my dream—served to elevate my spirits from my own *pity party* to find my own 'unstoppable' desire to be among the living. With this dream synchronicity (one that my RAS would have never allowed entrance into my inner nightclub without my dreams sneaking beneath the ropes while he was asleep) connected me to a higher frequency of thought that was medicinal to my *melancholy* heart.

One thing I know for sure is that with time everything becomes clear, all questions are answered, what's broken is restored, new trails are blazed, hearts are mended, love returns, and you will look over your shoulder, with a tear in your eye, at life's utter perfection.

Mike Dooley (TUT, The Universe)

Kelly shared another incredible true story about one of her clients *Saved By the Light*.

Ok, let's get to the business of *remembering* who we are and why we are here.

- Could there be a more important time in history than this to wake up?

- Could there be a more important time to dream a new dream for your life?

- Could there be a more important time in your personal history than this to remember the truth of who you are?

Dannion Brinkley is the author of the New York Times Bestselling book, *Saved by the Light*. Dannion has died three times, come back to tell the tale, and is known affectionately as "Dr. Death." He teaches that we all have a "holographic life review" that happens when we die. He says we all get to experience our lives in vivid detail from an omniscient point of view; the perspective of the person on the receiving end of our interactions; and through the eyes of someone who unconditionally loves us.

"This process," reports Brinkley, "straightens you right out. It means from that moment you have your life review, if given the opportunity to interact once again as a human, all you will want to do is to be kind, generous, appreciative, and loving to everyone you encounter...including yourself."

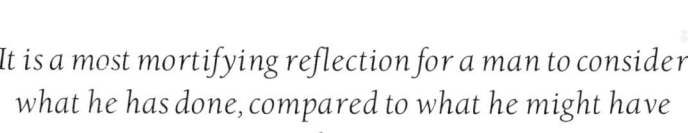

It is a most mortifying reflection for a man to consider what he has done, compared to what he might have done.

Samuel Johnson

In a bizarre series of dreams I repetitively was shown my life review, as if I had died. I was shown real-life scenarios where I had, in deed, chosen the high road. However, most of my life review illumined where I had *not* chosen the highest road...and the consequences of my words and actions on the people around me... most of which, I had never previously been aware or even considered.

For example, on my first day of junior high school, I was eleven years old, gangly, awkward, feeing too tall, and more than a bit klutzy. It was my great desire to be cool, and I tried with all my might to "act as if." My attempts to act cool got the attention of a group of older girls and before I knew it, I was surrounded by a heard of popular 8th grade girls (ala the movie, "Mean Girls".) They called me a series of four letter words I had never heard before—but I could tell by their faces and body language that it wasn't good.

Shaking and fearing I would throw up, I somehow pulled off the acting role of a lifetime and pretended to be unfazed, sarcastic, and holier than thou. *"Really? All of you 8th graders are ganging up on one 6th grader. How pathetic. You must feel really tough. Wow I'm impressed."* With that, I flipped my hair, walked away as if I was God's gift to the world...as if those tough girls were nothing more than pesky mosquitoes.

I always marveled at how I handled that moment (and the many other moments that followed.) I was impressed at my ability to have come up with a coping mechanism for surviving junior high without getting beaten up—by fooling those girls into thinking I was a Pit bull when I was really a quivering Chihuahua.

However, in my dreamtime life review I saw an entirely different movie possibility. I saw that had I been in a state of *Remembrance,* plugged in to source, illumined with the awareness of being flooded by all the love in the universe, I would have seen how afraid the "mean girls" actually were beneath *their* bravado. I might have seen how they had been abused and that they were, in fact, compensating for their own pain and lack of self-worth. Had I seen this, I might have embraced them, reassured them of their beauty, preciousness, their true identity as one with the divine.

Ok, this might have been a tall order to expect from a sixth-grader. However, in the realm of infinite possibilities, it was an available option...one I wish I had chosen. I continued reviewing my life from the vantage point of being completely awake. It was quite a different life experience, in deed. When I finally awoke from the last life-review dream in this series I felt I had lived the last scene from the movie "Groundhog's Day." Feeling inspired, I set a Declaration to live, to the best of my ability, from this moment forward, as awake as possible.

What if we don't have to wait until we die to have a holographic life review? What if we don't have to pray to have a dream wherein we had a life review? What if we didn't have to hit rock bottom and want to jump off a bridge to have our personal "Clarence" divinely intervene to help us remember who we are? Perhaps, if we choose, we can have a life review now. Why not? Why put off 'til we're on the other side what would benefit us now?

There's nothing in this world that encapsulates the message of how to 'awaken' more than the Prayer of Saint Francis. Whenever I've heard this prayer, no matter how asleep I might be it startles me awake. I hope it startles you back into the remembrance of the truth of who you are...not as a "getter", but as one at the center of the source itself...a true giver of all that you desire to receive:

Lord, make me an instrument of your peace,

Where there is hatred, let me sow love;

where there is injury, pardon;

where there is doubt, faith;

where there is despair, hope;

where there is darkness, light;

where there is sadness, joy;

O Divine Master, grant that I may not so much seek to be consoled as to console;

to be understood as to understand;

to be loved as to love.

For it is in giving that we receive;

it is in pardoning that we are pardoned;

and it is in dying that we are born to eternal life.

For-GET & For-GIVE

When I have forgiven myself and remembered who I am,
I will bless everyone and everything I see.

A Course in Miracles

For a moment, take the definitions you normally associate with the words *forgetting* and *forgiving*, and toss them aside. Become open to new definitions.

As I experienced in my Dreamtime Life-Review, when I was "sleep-walking", and asleep to who I really was, I related to myself as an "empty bucket," constantly seeking approval, protection, security, love, validation (fill in the blanks.) The empty bucket way of being caused me to be in full throttle taking, hoarding, protecting, and "getting" mode. In other words, when I/we relate to ourselves from a state of illusion, of having an empty bucket, then our lives are "for GETTING" (for-getting.)

Conversely, the state *Remembrance* is a plug for the hole in the bucket. When we are awake and remembering who we truly are, we are in a state of genuine seeing with pure aware-ness, receiving to the degree that our bucket is overflowing with well-being, abundance, wisdom, and source-energy to share. In a state of Remembrance our lives are dedicated to service, sharing, gifting, and uplifting. When we *re-member* who and what we are, we can't help but share from the overflow of our being, and our lives are "for GIVING" (for-giving.) We realize the more we give, the more we re-ceive.

When we are awake, we realize the pure bliss in life is in re-minding the people who have "for-gotten" who they are and that they are whole, perfect, and complete and they are utterly, "for-given" (in all aspects of the word.)

Consider for a moment the traditional meaning of the word "forgiveness." Perhaps the only thing to be "for-given" is how we behave when we fall asleep and for-get who we really are. But just like an appliance that is unplugged and cannot function as it is designed to, when we are unplugged from our source, the lights may appear to be on, but no one is home. However, just like when a toaster is plugged into an electric socket—without great deliberation about whether or not the appliance is worthy—the electricity begins to surge and the toaster can toast, the blender can blend, and the human can act humane...shining, beaming, in the way it was designed.

When you look without grasping, the whole universe is looking out of your eyes. It's an opportunity to see what it is to move without a sense of a central 'me.'

Mukti

Lessons learned from Chapter 8

1. Do you have a pet or loved one that has passed on? Would you like to make a connection? Pay attention to your dreams and get a dream journal. Keep the journal by your bed and when you wake up try to stay in the same position and calmly write what your dreams were about. You can share here what you learned?

    _____
    _____
    _____
    _____
    _____

2. Light a white candle and spend a few minutes asking God to help you connect with your loved ones on the other side. Ask that you have a visit and be very specific about who you would like to connect with?

    _____
    _____
    _____
    _____
    _____

Chapter 9

Chapter 9

CONCLUSION

... the journey never really ends

*"Life is not merely a series of accidents or coincidences
but rather a tapestry of events that culminate in an
exquisite sublime plan."*

Mashhur Anam

My life has been miraculous and I don't take one second for granted. I also don't believe in coincidences. I believe we are guided to people, circumstances, and situations that we can learn from. I will conclude this chapter with a series of events that led me to writing this book. I was struggling with having the confidence to share all my gifts I felt God nudging me to continue to write but I was still afraid of what people may think about it. I prayed and asked for some kind of sign for direction. These are the signs God gave me. I was over at my client's house; she and I have become very close and I share with her when I need encouragement. I told her about my fears of speaking the truth in my book. She said, "I have just the thing for you, it is the answer to your prayers." She handed me a book called, "When God winks".

When God Winks proposes that what we see as coincidences are really signals from God, reassurances that we are on the right path. Like winks from a loving parent, coincidences are mes-

sages from your Maker telling you that you are not alone and that everything will be okay. This compelling theory of why coincidences exist—and how to map them—is demonstrated by fascinating stories from history, sports, medicine, and relationships involving both everyday people and celebrities. Among the powerful messages is the idea that actions foster coincidences. It is possible to influence your future through prayer, visualization, and declaration. Add your own potential and unique gifts to the mix and you will begin to see signs of encouragement— winks from above that confirm that you're on the right track. It quite possibly could be one of the biggest reasons you are reading this book right now. GOD ALWAYS ANSWERS OUR PRAYERS. I wrote about that in my first book but reading this book was like having a personal conversation with God. I cried as I read story after story of how God winks. I highly recommend everyone read that book. I pray one day to meet the incredible author, Squire Rushnell and his beautiful wife, such an inspiration this book helped me write this book and share my divine message.

Some truly amazing things happened after I wrote my first book. You see it was an inspired writing which means it was divinely guided through me. I struggled with the idea of being so open and honest but God encouraged me to follow through. I am so grateful I did. In my first book, "Dogs are Gifts from God" I came out of the closet, so to speak with my spiritual gifts. I also shared about my traumatic childhood, teen years and my early adult years. It was so scary to be that raw and spiritually naked. My hands shook as I wrote each word. I was afraid of what people would think but it was my inner, authentic voice that told me that if I stepped out of my comfort zone; I would step into my dream zone. I knew this was the freedom I had longed for my entire life. I wrote every single word directly from my heart, I envisioned like-minded hearts reading my words and feeling their freedom. I trusted my guidance and published the book. It became a best-seller in animal rights.

I wanted to conquer my fear of public speaking. I decided to handle my fears and doubts the way I trained the dogs I worked with. I walked right up to what I was afraid of and the fear disappeared. I set my intention to be most helpful to animals and the idea to have my own radio show was placed in my heart. I was terrified in my first show but I stayed mindful and used all the strategies I have shared with you. I heard the word, 'WITH GOD ALL THINGS ARE POSSIBLE'. Something happened in that exact moment. I found my voice, I found my courage and strength; it had been inside of me all the time. My radio show was getting really popular, I felt unstoppable and I was so busy. My life had become all that I had dreamed about. People were calling me an expert. My business was growing and I had tons of speaking engagements. I thought this is it, I am a success. I have done it but something felt empty and I knew I was in for another lesson.

I was watching "Super Soul Sunday" on OWN network, I never miss it. I heard Brene Brown speak; it was as if she was talking directly to me, I felt so heard and acknowledged by what she was saying. She explained that there is a part of us, the shadow part or the inner critic that never feels we are good enough. I sat there thinking when will I be good enough? Will I be good enough when I am on Oprah or Ellen? Maybe I will be happy when I am a NY Times Best Seller? I realized in that moment and I screamed at the top of my lungs, I am enough and I am happy. A new sense of peace came over me .This is going to be a fun lesson; I can believe *in myself and quiet that inner critic. That day I started a journey into self-love and acceptance. I have never looked back. I am so grateful to Oprah and Brene that I turned on the television just in time to hear that.*

Oprah's next guest was Iyanla Vanzant she was such a powerful woman and she spoke about deep forgiveness. I knew it was time for me to truly forgive and accept myself. Then the commercial came on, it was "Soul Pancake" a truly inspiring group of videographers that want to make the world better. I wanted to learn more about this wonderful group and went to their website; www.soulpancake.com there was a video I watched an amazing story about Zach Sobiech; he was 17 years old and diagnosed with osteosarcoma, a rare form of bone cancer that takes the lives of a large percent of its childhood victims. Given only months to live, Zach turned to music to say goodbye. His song "Clouds" spread, and soon, Zach's message was heard across the country. Soul Pancake wanted to help Zach spread his message, and bring awareness to increase support for finding a cure. So, we asked our friends to help out...they did.

To download "clouds" and support Zach's Osteosarcoma fund:https://itunes.apple.com/us/album/clouds...

To support the Zach Sobiech osteosarcoma fund and help find a cure for childhood cancer visit: http://www.children-scancer.org/zach *This story touched my heart so deeply that I wanted to include this in my book. I know that Zach understands what life is really about and a beautiful BRIGHT light like his will never be extinguished. It made me think of Nate Berkus and how he survived a tsunami and shared with Oprah that he has turned up the volume on life and cherishes each precious moment.. I have learned this lesson and share it daily with my family friends, and clients. The Truth is none of us know how long they will be here in the physical form but we know life is about loving each other and learning while we are here. I am truly grateful for all these amazing teachers and I don't take anything for granted. I am so grateful for everyone in my life and I see the beauty and magic in every one and everything. It reminded me of my amazing nephew who started his own clothing line and community called "Inspired Emotion" It is clothes you wear to show you care. He prints positive statements on all types of apparel. My family is such a source of inspiration to me. I have the most amazing husband; we have been together for 19 years. We have a beautiful 17 year old daughter. I have an incredibly fulfilling business and I help make my corner of the world better. I was noticing how much I had to be grateful for and the freedom in that is wonderful.*

Oprah's next guest confirmed that for me Sarah Ban Breathnach; New York's Best Selling author of "Simple Abundance" she said, " More often than not, we discover who we are and what we love through revelations found in the ,simple, and the common. In tiny choices; in what seem like small changes. In the moments of quiet epiphanies when the static of the world clears; we realize the simple blessings in everyday life. The more we notice them the more blessings are found."

Just when I was feeling discouraged and didn't feel I had the strength or courage to write this book. The book by Wayne Dyer, "Wishes Fulfilled" fell off the book shelf at the library. I read that book and I applied everything I learned to write this book. Wayne says, "Wishes fulfilled" is designed to take you on the voyage of discovery, wherein you can begin to tap into the amazing manifesting powers that you possess within you and create a life in which all that you imagined for yourself becomes a present fact." When I read this book I decided to just sit and be still and let the book be written through me. I just needed to show up and trust the words I was inspired to share. I chose to accept this divine assignment and I know one day I will hug each of the people who I have written about in this book and in my first book. My mind and heart are completely open to receive the endless possibilities in store for me and the world. There is plenty for everyone including me. The book also talked about a wonderful woman Anita Moorjani talks about her near-death experience (NDE) and how it has transformed her—including her complete healing from end-stage cancer in the weeks following her NDE. In this hour-long conversation, Anita describes her experience on the Other Side, her return to this life, and her healing. She shares the truths she discovered about illness, healing, death, those who have passed on, the purpose of life, and who we truly are. Learn why there's nothing to forgive and why allowing love—unconditional self-love—is the key to moving forward into becoming who you were meant to be. Anita leads a guided meditation to access the very essence of your being and provides simple exercises to understand the nature of awareness and to begin living in the joy and magnificence that is your birthright.

In her truly inspirational memoir, "Dying to be Me" she relates how, after fighting cancer for almost four years, her body—overwhelmed by the malignant cells spreading throughout her system—began shutting down. *As her organs failed, she entered into an extraordinary near-death experience where she realized her inherent worth and the actual cause of her disease. Upon regaining consciousness, Anita found that her condition had improved so rapidly that she was able to be released from the hospital within weeks without a trace of cancer in her body!*

This reminded me of a time in my life, twelve years ago I was diagnosed with cervical cancer. At the time I was terrified but I found the experience to be a gift. I healed myself naturally and I learned how important it is to make myself a priority. The experience taught me that life is precious and not to take anything for granted. I learned that to live life to the fullest is by reaching out and help others whenever possible. Live your whole life in present awareness so that you know that you are always being guided, so your life becomes the meditation. Life is a gift and even though, your loved ones are no longer in the physical. Your loved one on the other side wants you to see your life as a gift. Whatever time you had with your loved one was your gift from them. Know that they are still with you and if you get quiet enough in your mind you will connect on a different level. I finally realized that the most important lesson to life is to be WHO you are to express your magnificence, don't deprive the Universe of what you came here to do. Your loved ones are just a thought away. You can connect with them; it is always your choice.

Another twist of faith happened and I knew that faith and love would be the only answer. My husband and I were sleeping in our home and our truck with our camper was parked in our driveway. During the night someone stole our truck and camper. Our family was devastated I was losing faith the police were not helping and I got on my knees and prayed I asked God to give me the strength and courage to believe it would all be okay. I began using all the principles in this book and an amazing thing happened my dear friend and client gave me a book by Joel Osteen called, "Live your Best Life yet" I read that book every minute I was afraid I remembered that God would help us and miracle after miracle happened. It felt like the whole community was rallying around us to help. We received support and love from strangers reaching out to help us in this difficult time. I knew it was God I could feel it and I knew WITH GOD ALL THINGS ARE POSSIBLE. I heard that statement over and over again it was amazing and another confirmation we are never alone. People in this world can do mean things to each other because we have freewill but faith and love are more powerful and can conquer even situations that seem impossible. Our truck was found and it was in perfect condition. I was so grateful to my friend who loaned me Joel Osteen's book. It comforted me and it helped me stay strong and believe God has my back.

I knew it was time for me to let go of the victim story that was not serving me. I am excited to share the divine message I was born to deliver. I am willing to be seen and vulnerable. I choose to shine my light so that others will shine their beautiful light. I am not playing small; I know that no one can deliver my message, only I can. I will stay in alignment with my divine message and speak for animals and children who are unable to speak for themselves. I am ready to be the powerful, strong woman I was born to be. I will remind myself often that someone's life will be changed, when I share my divine message. Oliver Wendell Holmes said that a mind, once stretched, never regains its original dimensions. I hope this book will open your mind to illuminate your perceptions and beliefs. With an open mind you can stretch to new dimensions of spiritual awareness. I pray that this book will change your life and that all your relationships improve. I hope you will stand with me because we are stronger together. This is the end of this book but please connect with me online. Help to create a No-Kill Nation for shelter animals. Become part of the solution. This is a new adventure and we are all part of the journey. I am here for you and look forward to hearing from you at www.positivelypetsandkids.com I hope you savor every moment with your dog and notice the divine in your canine, to apply the lessons that are provided daily. The exercises, meditations, and visualizations will transform your relationships, if you do them.

LET THE JOURNEY CONTINUE...............

> "A human being is a part of the whole called by us universe, a part limited in time and space. He experiences himself, his thoughts and feeling as something separated from the rest, a kind of optical delusion of his consciousness. This delusion is a kind of prison for us, restricting us to our personal desires and to affection for a few persons nearest to us. Our task must be to free ourselves from this prison by widening our circle of compassion to embrace all living creatures and the whole of nature in its beauty."
>
> - Albert Einstein

Lessons learned from Chapter 9

THE CONCLUSION

1. Do you have any stories about coincidences that you
    would like to share?

    _____

    _____

    _____

    _____

    _____

2. Are there any books you feel have been guided to you
    at a time when you really needed encouragement? List
    them here and pay attention to what is showing up in
    your like now that you are more aware of your thoughts,
    emotions, and feelings.

    _____

    _____

    _____

    _____

    _____

3. Take time to journal what you have learned from this book. Please track your success and challenges. You can also share on www.positivelypetsandkids.com

_____

_____

_____

_____

_____

Suggested Reading Section

The Four Agreements Companion Book by Don Miguel Ruiz
with Janet Mills published Hay House 2000

Wishes Fulfilled by Wayne Dyer published by Hay House 2012

The Everything Law of Attraction Book by Meera Lester
published by Adams Media 2008

Resurrecting Venus by Cynthia Occelli published Agape Media
2012

Your Best Life Yet by Joel Osteen published by Faithwords 2007

Dying to be Me by Anita Moorjani published by Hay House 2012

When God Winks by Squire Rushnell published by Thomas
Nelson 2006

Printed in Great Britain
by Amazon.co.uk, Ltd.,
Marston Gate.